THE INVISI3LES

Sexual Assault Awareness

ANTHOLOGY

DR. LASHONDA M. JACKSON-DEAN, DM, MBA, FAC-P/PM

Copyright © 2021 by Dr. LaShonda M. Jackson-Dean, DM, MBA, FAC-P/PM

The Invisibles Anthology: Sexual Assault Awareness

Jackson-Dean Investments Publishing

www.DrLaShondaJacksonDean.com

DrLaShondaJacksonDean@gmail.com

www.JacksonDeanInvestments.com

www.JustSoYouKnowMomentWithATwist.com

www.GreatnessPursued.org

All rights reserved. No part of this book may be reproduced, stored, in a retrieval system, or transmitted, in any form or by any means without written permission, from the original author Dr. LaShonda M. Jackson-Dean.

Each Co-Author is the sole owner of their individual literary work not collectively.

Printed in the United States of America.

Catalog-in-Publication Data for this book is available from the Library of Congress.

Library of Congress Control Number: In review

Book ISBN: 978-1-7337616-6

EBOOK ISBN - 978-1-7337616-7-3

Dr. LaShonda M. Jackson-Dean, DM, MBA, FAC-P/PM

Multi-Media Network Owner, TV Talk Show Host, Multiple National and International Best Seller Author,

Speaker, Transformational Coach, and Professor

www.DrLaShondaJacksonDean.com

Visit our online store for more books, promotional items, upcoming events.

Dedication

This Anthology is dedicated to the men and women who lived and relived the experience but yet, keep going.

For they understand that their strength, strengths and their stories of healing guides others to their own healing.

~ Dr. LaShonda M. Jackson-Dean

Acknowledgements

*We acknowledge the courage
it took for you to write your story, even if
you did not sign it. You shared your
strength for others to feel strong
enough to sign.*

#TheInvisibleWarriors

Contents

Preface	1
The Forbidden Dance	5
Learning to Steady My Aim	17
Stuck Like Chuck	27
Guppy Turned Piranha	39
The Secrets We Keep	51
A Life Restored	63
The Effects of Sexual Assault	77
Sexual Assault Assistance	81
References	83
Biographies	85
Meet the Authors	93

Preface

Nationally, April is Sexual Assault Awareness Month, making it imperative for this anthology to be published within this time frame. The annual observance is an opportunity to raise awareness as well to educate. The observance of the topic and many others allows for conversations to become teachable moments. When we are receptive to learning more about what we may fear, we give ourselves permission to grow as we learn.

Many are coping with the remnants of sexual assault through fighting silent battles of fear of public persecution. Leading to several sexual assault survivors not being comfortable with discussing the details concerning their experiences. There are always lingering feelings of being judged or even not believed, not to mention the reluctance of reliving the experience by talking about it. No two experiences are exactly, the same: where one person may find the discussion cathartic another may feel traumatized all over again. In this club where no one seeks membership, some accept assistance while others can't phantom how assistance could alleviate the pain, so they suffer alone.

Sexual assault is defined and described by several terms such as rape, desecration and defiled. Sexual assault can take on many forms to include: fondling or unwanted sexual touching, forcing a victim to perform sexual acts, such as oral sex or penetrating the perpetrator's body, attempted rape, and or penetration of the victim's body, i.e., rape. Rape is a form of sexual assault, but not all sexual assault is rape. Rape may be defined differently in different places, but the general definition includes unlawful, nonconsensual sexual intercourse or sexual penetration of a person's vagina, anus, or mouth by a perpetrator's sex organ, body part, or foreign object.

With the vast number of terms, the categories of the victims are just as broad. It is estimated that an American is sexually assaulted every 73 seconds. On average, there are 433,648 victims of rape and sexual assault each year in the United States (https://www.savacenterga.org/statistics). Sexual assault has no specific type as any race, ethnicity, background, gender, sexual orientation, and/or physical size have been reported. It can be perpetrated against men by women, man to man, woman to woman, and nonbinary people to nonbinary people. Which is why many of the names, dates, and some details have been modified in this anthology. In this case, the preference of being anonymous is understood and not mistaken as a hiding methodology. Personally, I see the act as a step forward in their recovery considering, they could have chosen to remain silent. These authors are not mere survivors...they are warriors.

The Forbidden Dance

The Forbidden Dance

By

Daisy Herman

I doubt I would have survived as long as I have had I remained the person I was before tragedy waltzed into my life. I refer to the incoming tragedy as a waltz because, my perpetrator literary swept me off my feet with his first impression. Being a young woman from meager means, I never received the spoils of life on a magnified level but what I did have made me feel rich. I came from a loving, close knit family, in a town where (Cheer's) everybody knew your name. I was raised with four of my siblings and a cousin by my grandparents. My mother never seemed to want to be a parent but magically kept getting pregnant. I never knew my father but, my grandparents made sure we all were loved. We never even missed our mother. A simple life and simple dreams until I started watching Dynasty.

I was amazed at all of the people who seemed to have so much and have it all together. It was much different from the life I was currently living. All of them had perfect teeth, perfect hair, the best body and so much money. Not having money was never a thought in their mind. I never really had thoughts about having money until I started fantasizing about having the life of a Carrington. Alexis Carrington was so confident and beautiful. With the snap of her fingers, she could have whatever she desired.

I found myself snapping my fingers and visualizing having everything I wanted. My thoughts elevated from watching the Carrington's, to wishing to be like the them to creating my own plan for upgrading my life. As I looked around my environment, my household, my family, friends, and even my town...no one was living the Carrington life. Even the white people considered to be the elite of the town appeared to only be fifty cent above everyone else. As white people, it was understood that our life was better than any of the Black people in our town but sometimes I wondered about that too. I would see a few of them in school but never really any where else. They always looked like they had everything they needed but...back to what I was saying.

> *My thoughts elevated from watching the Carrington's, to wishing to be like the them to creating my own plan for upgrading my life.*

No one in my immediate surroundings had what I had started believing I wanted for my life so I had no idea where to start. I began to see myself and my life differently every day. My stringy dishwater blonde hair no longer looked flowy. The freckles on my face were beginning to look more like a distraction and less like character. My eyes had no twinkle...where the hell did my twinkle go? I had never been on the slim side but not really what you call fat either... just, there. The funny thing about this was I was totally fine with all of this until I wanted to be better.

There have been times that I wondered if this is where my world went wrong. Maybe if I had stayed content in being who I already was and where I already was, maybe.....

I had to come up with a plan because I would be graduating from high school soon and I would have to start my own life. Being the oldest, I never had a big sister to model after of. To learn how to do my hair or make up. To copy the latest style in dressing or to even discuss boys with. I was as vanilla as it comes. Every week, I could not wait to watch the Carrington's on Dynasty. I began practicing my walk. I would sachet across the room into a complete spin. Oh, so much grace. So much beauty. Not me the characters on TV. As for me, I was a regular bull in the china cabinet which was why I was practicing...to become better. I believed that if I practiced long enough and hard enough, I would find my Blake.

I serious about changing my life for the better. I took some of the money I had been saving from my job at Handy's to buy a few improvements. I went to Fred's and purchased a sundress, face powder, mascara, lipstick, scented body lotion, and my first pair of high heeled shoes. I called it my Carrington. Every week, I would don my Carrington to watch the Carrington's. During commercials and after the show, I would practice my walk, my talk, and my dancing (picture Eunice from Moma's Family trying to be Alexis Carrington). I have to admit, I appeared to be getting better and better at this. Initially, I was unnoticeable to everyone I came in contact with. I was like a leaf on a pile of leaves. No one ever noticed anything about me or even initiated conversation with me and I was fine with this because, it had always been this way. I was shy and stayed to myself so I was kind of glad when I was not approached by anyone.

While working at Handy's one Friday at noon, I walked by a co-worker name Brock and after a minute, he ran up to me and inhaled deeply. This was completely shocking to me. I asked... Brock, what are you doing? Brock responded; you smell...really pretty. He wasn't Blake Carrington but his name did start with a B so, I was getting close. I blushed and walked swiftly away.

Well, if you guessed that my life hadn't truly improved you would be guessing correctly. I still had no real plan on how to upgrade my life until...I saw the Army commercial. "Be...all that you can be...in the Army." The light bulb in my head was overheating. I could not sleep thinking about going to see the Army recruiter the next day.

I went to the Minnesota Army Recruiter Station for information. I was told about the living arrangements, the training, the mission, the deployments, the guns, and the pay. I was surprised that pay actually came with all of this. I would have my own independence, my own place, my own job, my tuition, and my own money! I wanted to sign up that day but I had another year and a half in high school.

Fast forward to graduation. It was not my time to make decisions for myself. So, I quit my job at Handy's, kissed my grandparents and siblings goodbye. I chose the military as a way to improve my livelihood.

The Army life was three worlds of difference than the life I knew. I made it through the basic training and job training without dying, although, at times I thought I would. I met different people from all around the world and created friendships with those I would have never even said hello to in my home town. My first year in the Army taught me just how much in life I chose because of the way I was raised, to miss out on.

The time came for the Military Ball. I was so excited. I purchased my Army Mess Formal Uniform, went to the hair salon and put on makeup. I went to the event and everything was beautiful. I spoke to a few friends and just when I thought my night was good, it became grand.

As I prepared my plate at the buffet, I kept bumping hands with a man across from me. On the third bump, I looked up and said excuse me to a young, pimply face Corporal. Standing beside him was the most beautiful man I had ever seen... He was tall, blonde hair with the clearest blue eyes ever. We locked eyes and his smile brought me out of my star gaze and into a euphoric stare. He had perfect white teeth. He asked me if he could pour me a drink and I said I do.

Mr. Handsome God chuckled a little which slapped me back to reality and he asked me again. I responded yes, please. After he poured my drink, he ran his finger across my hand. Everything in me tingled and just like that he was gone. I never saw him again. Almost two years later, I met a guy that looked like him but I was not for sure considering I only saw him once but, he gave me the same feelings. Once again, we locked eyes and he walked over to me.... and walked past me.

He was tall, blonde hair with the clearest blue eyes ever. We locked eyes and his smile brought me out of my star gaze and into a euphoric stare.

I found myself thinking about him all day and every day. I went back to the eatery where I saw him but he was not there. He was probably my Blake and I had lost him before finding him so quickly. I would play over and over in my mind how we met, his eyes, his teeth, his cologne.

I was a workaholic. Anything that I did, I put my heart into it. I was eventually changed from the day time tour to the evening tour, which did not bother me much because I was not doing much at night besides sleeping. I had had a few dates, a boyfriend or two and some girl pals but nothing major. Just fun and experimenting. Sometimes, I went on dates. Sometimes, I went out with groups, and other times, I went out alone. After one of the group occasions, I was attacked on my way home. This day changed my life forever.

Everything happened so quickly. For the longest, all I could remember was being hit and knocked to the ground. My head hurt so bad and then everything went blank. Then next thing I could recall was feeling something in my mouth. I was then eye to eye with my attacker. I tried to move but the movement was only in my mind because I could no longer feel anything below my neck. My body was numb and lifeless. There I was looking into his eyes, and they were like an ocean, so blue. I tried to scream but no sound came out. He held his finger up to his mouth that was covered by his ski mask. He then rubbed his face across mine and then over my chest. He flipped me over. My face was now on the ground. He pulled my dress over my head and penetrated me from behind. It felt like forever came and went. I could not say or feel anything. I do remember tears rolling down my cheeks. He then muffled his moans into my back as we both collapsed to the ground. I laid there praying he was finished and I did not suffocate as my face pressed into the grass. He then flipped me over and started again...

He moved up to look me in my eyes again. He just stared at me while he assaulted me. I could not do anything to make him stop. I could not do anything to help myself. I could not save me. He got off me and left me there in a lifeless state. Seemed as if I had been there for hours before I was able to move. I finally gathered myself and looked around. I grabbed my purse and ran all the way home. Which was not very far. Once in my apartment, I walked cautiously to my bathroom. After being attacked, you always feel like there is someone else waiting to attack you. I was hoping he was not in my house. I showered and cried. I spent the next couple of days in the bed. I grabbed my purse and returned to my base to requested some time off. I realized my wallet was not in my purse. I could not remember the last time I had it. I received approval for my time off and left. I never told anyone what had happened.

When I was sexually assaulted, violated, defiled, my body was desecrated. When I was raped, I did not tell anyone because I did not think I could speak the words. I could not allow another person to take a piece of me from me. I could not bear the hurt, the pain, the judgement, the looks from others. I was supposed to be here getting my life together. I was supposed to be here working towards my Carrington life and finding my Blake but ....I am here getting sexually assaulted.

Just the thought of what I endured made me physically sick. I found myself being stressed, crying, sleepless nights, loss of appetite, increase of appetite, loss of weight, gaining of weight, my hair even fell out. I vomit at the thought of the incident. I found myself not wanting to have any sexual contact. I stopped seeing my "guy friend" because, I could not bear to tell him what had happed. I remembered thinking... just what I could have done in my life to deserve this? What could I have done to have caused such a horrific incident in my life?

What could I have done differently that night to change the outcome of this encounter? I also asked myself why did he select me?

After taking some time off, I returned to the base a totally different person. All of the confidence I had gained over the time I was in the military was stripped from me in one night. I had finally come out of my small-town girl shell to find my way...only to come to this. Everything I was experiencing were the inner me screaming for help but from where? How could I get help if I can not even admit that I was...that this had happened?

What could I have done to have caused such a horrific incident in my life? What could I have done differently that night to change the outcome of this encounter?

About a year later, I mustered up the strength to rejoin the world by going to a club with some friends. Happy to be out of the house, I was having a decent time until a familiar looking guy kept passing by me. I reminisced that it was my Blake I lost so many years back. From a distance, it looked like him, blonde, handsome. We locked eyes and he started walking towards me. I felt my body tingle and the closer he came the tingle turned into fear. There he was about three feet away and I noticed...the ocean in his eyes. He walked up and asked if there was something I would like to say? I was speechless. I subconsciously asked myself if this was my Blake? I then asked myself, if my Blake was also my attacker? Then he asked if I still lived in the same apartments. He then placed his finger in front of his lips as if to tell me to be quiet. I turned and ran to my car to go home.

As I drove home... I asked myself if this was what I asked for? Is this the life I thought was an improvement? The following week, I requested to transfer to a different Army base.

Dr. LaShonda M. Jackson-Dean

Over time, I found myself blaming myself for what he did to me. I also figured out how he knew where I lived. He had my wallet with my ID. I replayed the details of the event in my head night after night. I consider different scenarios of how things could have been different had I taken a taxi opposed to walking home. Differently, if I had not even gone out that night. I finally decided to seek assistance for my trauma.

The therapy has been hard. I had built up a defense mechanism of not thinking about what happened. This was the only thing that had helped me feel better. I had to remove it from my thoughts. My therapist makes it a point to make me relive the moments while in therapy, saying repression leads to denial. Even when I tried to deny it happened, I was well aware that it did and the thoughts are very painful. I have explained this to my therapist in several sessions but she still asks me to tell it again or write it out.

My story does not have to be your story or vice versa.

My personal thoughts on this are the event is too painful to relive over and over. I am not in denial, I fully aware of the realness of the event. I recognize this event to be the fracture between the person I used to be and the person I am now. The person I am now is stronger because she has to be. The person I am is wiser because I know what happens when I do not think ahead. The person I am is more cautious because I lived through what happened when I let my guard down. The person I am now does not trust that there is a Blake Carrington for me.

I believe people handle tragedy differently. Everyone has their own way of living through the events. We also handle the effects of tragedy differently. We should never admonish another person for doing what they consider best for them because we do not understand their reasoning. Honestly, it's not for us to always understand why people respond the way that they do. It should also not be our responsibility to try to figure it out. My story does not have to be your story or vice versa. If you have experienced a sexual assault or harassment, I recommend that you seek professional assistance. When I think back over the years, my life may have been different had I asked for help after I was assaulted.

~

Primary Author Conclusions:

In this chapter, the underlying subject is determining how one would recognize a person intending to sexually assault or rape a person. Though not always initially known, the majority of sexual assaults and rapes are committed by person or persons known by the victim. Most would like to believe that no one we know would do such a thing but despite popular belief the perpetrators are not always a stranger. This is why we must be careful in creating perceived public imagery of what an assaulter or rapist looks like, as well as, what we perceive rape to be. There may be similarities in different cases but none are identical. When all the information is released, no sexual assault experience is seen the same by the victim and the public. Their experience is not what society thinks rape looks like.

It should also be acknowledged that stopping rape is never the responsibility of the victim. The responsibility should lie among the person committing the assault. To believe so would place the potential victim or victim to live in a world of constant fear, caution, and suspicion. This would be unfair for anyone.

THE INVISIBLES

Learning to Steady My Aim

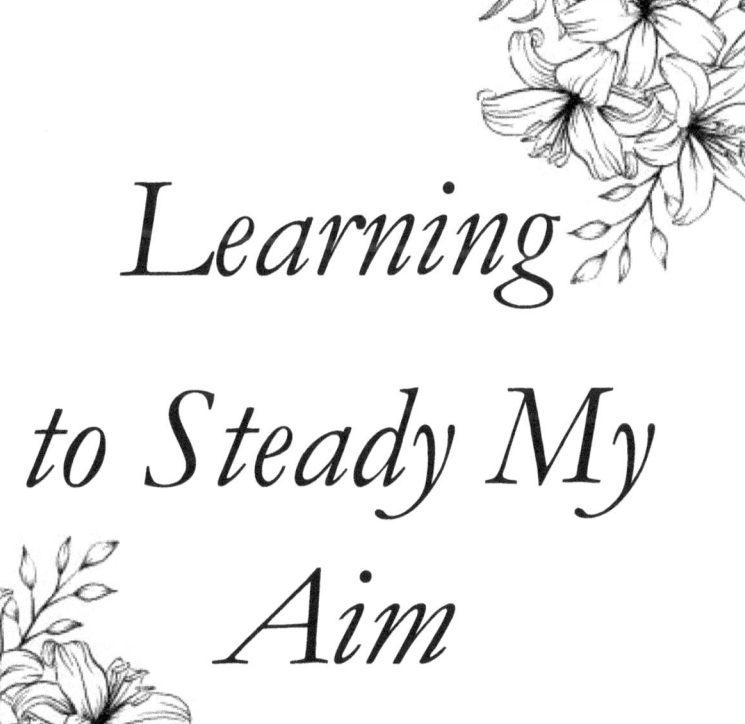

Learning to Steady My Aim

By

Dr. LaShonda M. Jackson-Dean

There was a time in my life that I could barely stand my own reflection. I asked myself, "How did I get here? How did I find myself in this type of position?" I was a new Airman in the United States Airforce, still in the midst of getting to know who I was as a military person, as well as, getting to know the people in my new family; my military brothers and sisters. This was a totally different life for me. Being a person who never felt the need to t in, everything about the military was so uniform with conformity. I witnessed my comrades fail several times trying to adapt to the common goal of the military. I could have been a member of that same group but because I decided that my "why" was more important than my need for individuality, I made it through military boot camp. I was determined to get money for college and have my own life. Graduation came and I was so proud. Goal set, did the work required, and success was achieved. Little did I know that this would only be the first of many goals to come.

Dr. LaShonda M. Jackson-Dean

> **I was determined to get money for college and have my own life.**

At this point in my military career, freedom was more permissible, paving the way for my individual persona to return. Just like the regular world, there were cliques and groups within the ranks and just like the regular world, this did not bother me. I have always danced to my own tune, and being the band, I created the beat I danced too. This made me very interesting to many. I received several invites to several events that I took no interest in, but the invites kept coming. Midway through my first year, I received an invite in person. I heard someone say she's not going to come, she never does. For some reason, I took this as a personal dare. As I looked around, no one was representative of the person I was, the type of people I would normally socialize with, or the activities I would partake in but I was not perfect either so, I did not want to judge. I agreed to attend a party with people I did not really know because I did not want them to see me as being predictable. This one night would be the beginning of many nightmares for the next twenty or more years. I entered the party, located at a hotel, to be precise, a hotel suite. Everyone seemed to be enjoying themselves. I was poured a drink and I accepted it. In normal situations, I would have never taken a prepared drink from someone I did not know but, on this night, I did. This is where my life changed forever.

My last clear thought that I remember from that night was sitting on a couch listening to someone's story. From that point, everything was like an out of focus video. I could hear people having fun, chatting and laughing. I could see people walking back and forth until people in the room became fewer and fewer but, I could not get off of the couch. Everything from this point resembled clips of the unfocused videos. When I finally gained full consciousness, to my horrid dismay, I realized I had been sexually assaulted.

THE INVISIBLES

From this one night, my persona went from a confident woman with full self-awareness and a great life ahead of her, to a recluse.

I was filled with doubt, shame, guilt and was now clinically depressed. I lost my high self-esteem, my confidence and my will to do anything more than just exist. At first, besides the obvious and what I could physically see, I was unsure of everything that had transpired that night. I simply wanted to disappear. On two occasions, I took pills with the hope of not waking up but, like clockwork, I would. Considering I was still in the military, there was no time to procrastinate getting to the base.

I was filled with doubt, shame, guilt and was now clinically depressed.

I had to report in and simply not showing up was out of the question, so I did. I was met with strange jeers, whispers and stares. I was not sure if it was coming from people who attended the party or from those who were told of the occurrence. I became angry. I had to constantly remind myself why I did not call the police and why I refused to tell anyone what happened to me. The truth was, I did not know all that happened to me and more so, who did it to me. What I did feel was, I was the cause of it all. Why did I go? Why didn't I call the police? Why did I shower away all of the evidence? Why do I have all these questions now that I have closed myself away from the rest of the world? My world involved me doing what I had to do (reporting in at the Air Base) and coming home. I kept my apartment dark. I did not socialize beyond what was necessary. I felt damaged. I felt alone. I could not talk about the incident because I was too embarrassed to admit what happened. I was slowly dying side. I promised myself that I would never fall victim to anything such as this again. This continued for years. I did everything I could to break out of that funk but it had a death grip on my life. My breakthrough did not come until I began to accept the things that I could not change. The main thing that I could not change was the thing that was holding me hostage; I was a rape victim.

I said it. My heart dropped. I felt myself sink to the floor and I laid there and cried. I cried until I could not cry any more. I then heard my own thoughts ask me, "Now what?" I got off the floor, got on my knees and prayed. Every day, I would get on my knees and pray for healing, then I prayed for wisdom, then understanding. The last thing I prayed for was recovery. I received all of what I asked for in that order.

My breakthrough did not come until I began to accept the things that I could not change.

Fast forward through obtaining a few degrees, several certifications, accolades, successful businesses, marriage and children, I had made it through. I made it through with prayer and I finally remembered who I was. I finally got out of my own way which was holding me hostage in a situation I had no control over. Would I have been the person I am today without this traumatic experience?

I can neither confirm or deny this, but I do feel it was definitely an awakening of my spirit. Before the incident, I could either see or not see things or instances, depending on the situation. The incident that happened that night changed that in me. As horrid as it was, it caused me to become more aware of my surroundings and the participants in my environment. Being more aware has trained my focus and assisted me in several business deals. I continued on to earn my Bachelors, MBA, my Doctorate degree and several high-level certifications. Through it all, my path continued to lead me towards service and assisting others. Whether it is through mentorship, coaching, or simply supporting, I have always prided myself in helping others become more successful.

THE INVISIBLES

I am Dr. LaShonda Jackson-Dean, CEO of Jackson-Dean Investments, the parent company of several other businesses including Jackson-Dean Professional Solutions; a life coaching practice for professional women. I also provide coaching services through my non-profit organization, Greatness Pursued, to women having difficulty in their transition from military to civilian life. The majority of these women also suer from Military Sexual Trauma (MST). Under my leadership, Greatness Pursued has provided a safe place for the coaching of hundreds of women and provided basic living necessities for over three hundred other Veterans.

I am an author of eight published books: A Phenomenological Study of the Underrepresentation of Senior Level African American Women in Corporations, Seed to Seeds Systemic Oppression and PTSD, Level Up! Through Mindfulness, Level Up! Through Mindfulness Life-Book Part II, A Tea Party and a Prayer (Children's Book), The PIVOT Anthology, The Christmas Magic of You, and now, The Invisibles: Sexual Assault Awareness. Future works include The Adventures of Tike and Tunka (Children's Books) and The Invisibles (the 4 parts of the 5-Part Series). I have participated in five collaborations, Gumbo for The Soul: Liberating Memoirs and Stories to Inspire Females of Color, Love Letters for My Girls, and Women Win Against the Odds, I'm Speaking: Rewritten Rules Of Encouragement To Affirm Women Disruptors, with another one in the works entitled Break-Through. I am also a Multiple National and International Best-Seller Author as well as, a Multiple National and International Empowerment Speaker.

With the plethora of hats, I have worn and currently wear, the moniker that stands out the most is The TV Talk Show Queen! The name was coined after I took the talk show world by storm with my show Just So You Know Moment with a #Twist TV Talk Show.

I never planned on my TV career ending with the one show so I took it to the next level. I, Dr. LaShonda M. Jackson-Dean, am now the owner and producer of JDI Multi-Media Network. Always looking for ways to share my servant leadership style, I created my network with others in mind and subsequently it has led to profits. My network provides a platform for creating media opportunities for aspiring producers. The JDI Multi-Media Network offers something that most networks fail to consider; creative independence. The network has exclusive genres with the air of open mic ability. The JDI Multi-Media Network welcomes creators and producers interested in using television as a medium for conveying their message to the world. The JDI Multi-Media Network uses mass communication to include digital streaming as well as, social media platforms.

To think I almost let go. I almost gave up on any and everything that could have possibly been.

Some will enter their seasons and reach their time at different moments and that is fine

I almost threw in the towel myself. I know now that my breakthrough was not important only for me, but for others as well. Had I stayed on the floor waddling in my tears and regret, I would have forfeited the opportunity to coach other women through their trials. They needed me to get better too. To think I allowed an incident that I had no control over to control me. I allowed a traumatic experience to dictate my response to everything around me. This inflicted trauma tricked me into believing that I was less because of it. I wore a scarlet letter towards the public that didn't even know what it was for. I punished myself for a crime I did not consent to.

This was indeed a trying time in my life but I finally woke up to live past my trauma. I had to finally realize that there was no calvary coming to save me. I had to decide to go to Calvary for my salvation. Through my own personal expedition, the purpose for my life was restored. This restored purpose caused an awakening in me that I want to share with others. For everything, there is a time and a season. Some will enter their seasons and reach their time at different moments and that is ne. There will be incidents in our lives that cause us to shut down, but they will teach us that we all respond differently to trauma and things that hurt us.

I learned that negative experiences, despite how traumatic they are, you can overcome them. We can live again. For those reading my story who feel they cannot move forward, please know that if I can learn to steady my aim to produce greatness out of my bad experiences, you can too.

Stuck Like Chuck

Stuck Like Chuck

By
Marjorie Calhoun

I remember my senior year in high school, during that time, what else could I have done? Young, essentially dumb, no money, no job, and barely a high school education. Now, I am pregnant and having to tell my parents. I decided to elope because I did not want to hear the disappointment in their voices because they were expecting so much of me. I was supposed to be the one who would make it. I would be the one who would go to college and make something of myself. I would be the educated family member that would get a good job and would be able to send money back home to help out. I would be the one that my parents would get to brag to their friends about. They had my life all planned out.....let's just say, it didn't exactly go that way.

Fast forward (30) thirty years...I was simply living life and minding my own business. I was not even looking for companionship, I was just in search of myself. I had been in a marriage since I was seventeen years old. I married my high school sweetheart because we were in love...and had a baby on the way. I was a good wife and by the age of (24) twenty-four, the mother to our six children (two sets of twins). My husband worked a full-time job and paid all of the bills. He never accepted that I wanted to work. I really

Marjorie Calhoun

felt like he kept me pregnant to keep me from working. I was finally able to get a secret part-time job when I got the last baby in school. I worked as a sitter for an elderly couple for a few hours a day. I figured out a way to get my husband up and out to work, get the children ready and to school and then make it to my job. I was always caring for someone.

> *I remember praying to God to help me get the unstuck but there I was stuck. It was getting later and I had no other choice but to call my husband.*

I still remember... it was a rainy day and like always, I had gotten everyone off to their respected places for the day. I went to my job as well but had trouble leaving because of the rain. My car got stuck in my client's yard and I could not get out. I continued trying to drive out and the tire kept sinking deeper in the mud but, I had to get home before my husband. I remember praying to God to help me get the unstuck but there I was stuck. It was getting later and I had no other choice but to call my husband.

I called my husband Charles and gave him the details of my plight. He just sat on the phone for a minute and then asked where was I and why was I there. I told him that I had stopped to check on an elderly couple I knew and had gotten stuck. Charles was quiet for about a minute and then he said "I'm on my way". Whew! That was close.

I waited in the house with my clients until I thought Charles would be arriving, I then sat in the car. Charles pulled up with some boards and strategically placed them behind the tire. Within ten minus tops, my car was unstuck. I looked aback towards the house as I reversed out the yard and noticed my client's husband standing with my husband waving good bye. I heart sunk and I had the feeling I was stuck again.

THE INVISIBLES

I saw our children in our yard as I parked the car, with Charles behind me. I ushered them into the house and started working on dinner. I got the children started on their homework and ran a bath for Charles. I was so glad to be home. I stood in the bathroom mirror fixing my hair, I was a true beauty in those days. Charles walked in the bathroom as I turned the bath water off. He asked me why I was at the elderly couple's home. I repeated what I told him on the phone. He asked me if, I was sure? Before I could finish responding yes, he had slapped me across my face.

This was the first time Charles had ever put his hands on me. I was in utter disbelief.

This was the first time Charles had ever put his hands on me. I was in utter disbelief. Charles proceeded to tell me that my client's husband had told him that I took care of them everyday and I would be back tomorrow. Charles told him I would not because I quit. I asked him why he would tell them that? I expressed that he could not do that because I was a grown woman and this was my job. Charles released another slap across my face. He then said, he was the bread winner in our household and he did not need my help to take care of his family. He told me that I had insulted him and disobeyed him. He told me I was not to return to my job.

The next day, I continued as usual with the exception of going to my job. I sat on the couch to watch TV but all I could think about was my clients. I know they were waiting for breakfast and for their medications and I was not there to give it to them. I grabbed my keys and went to work. I hurried through my day and got back home. My days went this way for a period of time. Two years later, my client's husband had a heart attack and died. Charles and I attended the funeral. I wanted to go alone but Charles was adamant about going with me.

Marjorie Calhoun

After the funeral, my client's daughter walked up to me and gave me an envelope. She then said, my siblings and I want to thank you for always taking good care of our parents in our absence. We don't know what we would do without you considering we all live out of the area. I could feel Charles's blood boiling. Charles and I did not speak to each other all the way home. When we got in the house, I sat on the couch to watch TV. I called for the children but they were leaving to hang with friends. As soon as the door closed behind them as they left, I heard Charles say, "How could you do this to me?" I begged him to let me explain. Charles not only slapped me but he beat me that day. I decided that day that when the youngest child graduated, I was divorcing Charles.

I quit my job. I stayed around the house all day being Suzy Home Maker. Everything went back to normal...well sort of. Charles never hit me again. I was doing all of the things that I would normally do but, I was not myself. I was sad. I did this for years. I ensure Charles was up and ready for work. I ensured the children were up and off to school. I kissed everyone at the door.

> *I could feel Charles's blood boiling. Charles and I did not speak to each other all the way home.*

I welcomed everyone home. I started dinner. I got the children started on their homework. I ran a bath for Charles. I did this until all of my children were in college with the exception of one. We now had one child left at home. I was x-ing off the days to his high school graduation and first day of college!

On our youngest child first day of college, I packed my clothes and left home while Charles was at work. I went to a hotel. The next day, I found me an apartment and a job. By the third day, I was pulled over by the police. I was asked if I owned the car I was driving. I said yes. I was then told that the car had been reported stole and the driver possibly kidnapped. I assured him I was fine and I was the owner. The police asked me was I in any danger. I told him no and that I had decided to leave. At this point, he must have believed I was having a mental episode and Charles was called.

Charles drove up and hugged me. He was sobbing uncontrollably and thanking the police for "finding" me. I expressed to the both of them that I was not lost, I was in my full mental capacity, and I was leaving. Charles asked me why? The police asked if we would be ok if he left? We both said we would be. Charles and I stood there and talked. I told him how he made me feel when he forbade me to work and when he fought me. Charles begged me to forgive him. He told me that he just wanted to be the one who took care of me. He then begged me to come home. I told Charles that I had just gotten me an apartment and a job. I then told him that I was filing for divorce. I could see the hurt in his eyes. He walked back to his car and sat there. I got in my car and went to my new home.

I walked in my empty apartment and I felt so liberated! I bought a sheet set and comforter and slept on the floor that night. I felt good but different. I felt different but scared. I felt scared but free. The next day I went to work. After work, I came home. While going into my apartment, I thought I saw Charles drive by. The next day I had furniture delivered to my apartment. As the delivers brought my new furniture in, I saw Charles drive by. I figured it was time I told the children. I called them and received absolute rejection to the idea of divorce. Our children had never witnessed any of the abuse nor did they know about the job. I explained it all but each one questioned me as if I was lying. One after the other asked "When?" When Mom?" When did all of this happen?" I got to the point where I gave up trying to explain. For one, they did not believe it and for two, I did not want them to think I was just bad mouthing their father. The following week, I filed for divorce.

> *Charles begged me to forgive him. He told me that he just wanted to be the one who took care of me.*

Three weeks later Charles came by. I opened the door and asked him what he wanted. He told he was there to ask me back one more time or to sign the divorce papers with me. I told him that we could sign the papers. He asked if he could come in to talk. I allowed him to enter. We talked about our marriage. We talked about our children. We talked about our life together. Charles told me he did his best to care for our family and asked if I believed him. I agreed. I told him that was not the issue. The issue was I felt like a prisoner in our marriage and I simply needed to get unstuck. Charles said "Unstuck?" Then he repeated it "Unstuck?" he then said Woman, how were you stuck? I took care of everything including you and the children. You had nothing to worry about, all you had to do was keep the house and keep everyone in line. Even when you could not do that, I took up the slack by cooking or getting the children in line. What else could you have possibly wanted? I responded that I wanted me.

Charles began to sob. He asked me why we were not enough for me? I could not answer his question. So, I stood up and asked if he was ready to sign the divorce papers? Charles stood up and open his arm for a hug. I could see the pain on his face and I just wanted to make it go away. I reached out to him and we embraced each other. I knew Charles still loved me because I still loved him. As we embraced each other, we began to kiss. We kissed passionately. Charles held me tighter and I remembered how good his embrace was. I felt myself falling for him all over again. I had to stop this.

I told Charles that we were going about this the wrong way and that I had already made mind up. I asked him to sign the paper work. Charles looked at me as said can we give it another week? What's the rush? We have been together our whole life. We do not have to rush this. I agreed. Charles got his hat and left.

As the week went on, Charles called me every day when he woke up, at his lunch time, when he made it home and before he went to bed. With every call, he reminded me I was still his wife and he wanted me to come home. With every call I explained to him that I was not coming home and I needed to do this for me. Three weeks passed by and we still had not signed the divorced papers. Charles invited me out to dinner. I declined. Charles showed up at my door with dinner and roses. I let him in. We had a wonderful dinner with wine. After dinner we sat on the couch and watched TV. It was hard to distinguish if this was a date or just us....

Neither of us were drinkers and the wine had us a little tipsy. I fell asleep on the couch as we watched TV. I was awakened to Charles having sex with me. I yelled for him to stop and attempted to push him off me. I could not. He would not listen to my pleas either. Charles reminded me that I was still his wife and he was still my husband.

Charles begged me to forgive him. He told me that he just wanted to be the one who took care of me

I felt conflicted in the matter. He was right. He was still my husband and I was still his wife. Regardless of the fact that I had left him a month or so earlier, we were still married. I was also conflicted as to whether I was enjoying this or was I repulsed? Were we making love or was he sexually assaulting me? Was this rape? Is my husband raping me? Can a wife be raped by her husband? These were the thoughts in my head.... After Charles released inside me, he kissed me ever so gently and went to sleep.

I was now in a world of confusion because I did not know what to feel at that moment. I did not know whether I had been raped or had consensual sex? All I knew was...my husband was a sleep on my couch and I had let him in. I began to cry and pace. Pace and cry. I went to bedroom and laid across my bed and sobbed. Sometime later Charles came in my bedroom and told me to start packing my things because I was coming home. I said no. Charles ran his hand through my hair and said yes, you are. I then asked him to leave. Charles walked to the other side of the bed and got under the covers. I could not believe what was happening. At this point I did not know what to do, so, I just laid there.

The next morning, I woke up to the smell of breakfast. I guess I had forgotten about the previous night because I felt rather good. Charles brought me breakfast in bed. He kissed me on my forehead and told me he had already stared packing things. It was then that the memory of the night before came crashing back on me. Sitting there with the plate of food in my lap, I felt shell shocked. Charles said "eat your breakfast because we have a long day a head of us." I looked at him. He said, "we have to get this place packed up." I said no. I am not going anywhere. Charles just smiled and handed me a glass of orange juice. He kissed me on my neck. I turned to Charles and said "you need to leave." "I am not going back to your house." "This is my house. I am staying here and I am divorcing you." "Last night was a mistake." "I told you no and you persisted." "I did not want to have sex with you and I did not consent." Charles said, "Well, did you consent to what we did this morning?" "You climbed on top of me and got me to have sex with you this morning." Before I could deny it, I remembered doing it. So, there I was... stuck again. Charles took my plate away and proceeded to have sex with me again. I did not resist because I felt I had already lost the battle. I just endured it.

THE INVISIBLES

I did not know whether I had been raped or had consensual sex?

I did not move back in with Charles and I threaten him into signing the divorce papers about two weeks later. I really believed he signed because he had grown tired of my rejection. We are still participating in our children lives as a family but not as a married couple. I am seeing a therapist and was told that I had indeed been raped. I learned through my therapist that no is still no even with your spouse. My therapist asked me if I wanted to file charges and I declined. I explained this to Charles and he kissed me on my forehead and said he disagreed.

I continued to see my therapist not because of the rape issues but because of the confliction of my feelings about the incident. My confliction is so deep, I have refused to call it rape because I believe I may have subconsciously consented to the act.

~

Primary Author's Conclusions:

In this chapter, the matter of the legality of spousal rape. One may ask the question of whether rape can occur between a married couple, the answer is yes. This goes back to the definition above consent is having an affirmed agreement regarding sexual activity. In this case, married couples are assumed to have sexual engagement on a regular basis but it does not mean that marital rape does not exist. According to one study, "Approximately 10-14% of married women are raped by their husbands in the United States" (Bergen and Barnhill, 2006).

Sexual assault and/or rape constitutes any nonconsensual sexual intercourse—between non-spouses has always been illegal. However, until 1975, every state had a "marital exemption" that allowed a husband to rape his wife without fear of legal consequences.... Since

1993, all 50 states and DC have enacted laws against marital rape (McMahon-Howard, Clay-Warner, and Renzulli, L. 2009).

In my opinion, there is no difference between Marital sexual assault and/or rape or any other forms of sexual violence. All acts are serious and should be treated as such. Being in a situation where a person feels they are obligated to have sexual activity with another person poses a tremendous burden. This may also place them in an unsafe environment. In either one of these predicaments, the ability to consent has been removed along with the obligation.

Guppy to Piranha

Guppy Turned Piranha

By

Channel Austin

I now realize that I did not ask for any of this to happen to me. I now realize that I am the victim in this. I now realize that none of it was my fault. I have come to realize that what happened to me invaded my life and not the other way around. I have also come to realize that the guppy was never meant to grow into a piranha and this was not my fault either. I do not accept responsibility for anything that was birth from the sexual assault that I experienced that hot summer day in Monroe, Louisiana.

I consider myself as being a very giving individual. I truly believe others would say the same if they are honest. I give because I know what it feels like to not have and need. I share because I know what it feels like when things are held from you. I include because I know what it feels like to not be included. I love hard because I know what it feels like to not feel loved.

One would think the experience of lack of love would come from a person who had no one available. I wish this was the case. I have always had plenty of people around me being the third child in a

Channel Austin

family of eight children but I never received the love I needed from my family. I received just enough to say I received something.

Not frilly, no want or need for make-up, just comfortable with my bare face and ponytail. I believe my issues started when I traded my ponytail for a tapered fade. My reasoning, not that I feel the need to explain myself was that I liked to play basketball. A lot of hair and sports do not go together, unless you intend on washing your hair after every game. I was not blessed with the whole washing and go hair texture. When I wash my hair, there is a process and time to accomplish this. So, I chose sports over hair troubles. This offered me simplicity but suspicion came with it.

Let me go back.... Prior to the bald fade, I was a cute face, plain dressing young lady who enjoyed being around people but did not have a lot of friends. I did not have a lot of friends because of my low tolerance for the games people play that are not sports. I have been around people who smile at each other long enough for them to leave, then they talk bad about them.

I would see this happen time and time again util one day I spoke up. I told the group they were wrong for doing what they were doing. I also pointed out to each one who was talking about who. They were shocked but they recovered and continued as they normally did...only without me. You see, they were comfortable with each other because they were one in the same. I ended up being shocked because they were mad at me for speaking up.

I was shocked but not to the point of disbelief because I had already seen they were crooks. They had an honor code among them to be what they were... crooks. From this, I never had a lot

I include because, I know what it feels like to not be included. I love hard because I know what it feels like to not feel loved.

of female friends often, more male.

So, let's put their petty thoughts together to gauge their suspicion. No make-up. (check). No interest or participation in broken female syndrome games. (check). Plenty of basketball, warm-up shorts and sneakers. (check). No one officially knows who I date because I do not kiss and tell. (check). Traded long hair for a tapered bald-fade haircut. (check). I am sure you can figure out what the speculation is now.

From that point, all I heard was I suspect. Yes, I was now suspicious of being gay. Not that I have anything against the gay community and what they stand for, I am just not a participant. I have been labeled as such because of my appearance and the thoughts of others. I was not labeled because of who I actually am or anything I actually did but from what was thought.

These thoughts were not those of females alone, there were some males (who did not know me) thoughts as well. If things were said in my presence, I did not respond because I did not feel I needed to. I also felt that if they were not speaking to me directly, I cannot be for certain they were referring to me. Actually, I did not care what they thought or said. In reality, I had a boyfriend that I was happy with, who did not have an issue with my appearance.

I played basketball in the park every Saturday with different guys, some I knew and some I did not. On one Saturday, I played in several informal basketball pickup games, which lasted throughout the day. My team was winning the majority of the games played on Saturday.

During the games, there were a few guys being vocal on their thoughts of why my gaming techniques were so good. Their comments included that I should stop trying to be a dude. I should leave the game to guys. Along with those comments came name calling such as butch and manly. I felt compel to ensure I played my best to show them that my looks had no bearing on my performance.

Channel Austin

> **"** I responded, "Convert me from what to what?" He responded, "from a dike to a real woman." **"**

I was the only female on my team which was not uncommon an das I mentioned, I had more male friends than female friends. My team were the clear victors in this basketball event! There was plenty of trash talking (hood and sportsman vernacular) during and after the games to include sore loser verbal mental gymnastics.

I have to say I was feeling pretty good about the wins and may have let my guard down to low. To return home, I had to walk through the park to get to my street. While I was walking home, I saw a few of the guys riding their bikes passed me. I heard one of the guys say, "good game." I gave them a lay up move as my response (swish). Then I heard one of the guys yell... "Dike". I was disappointed by not surprised, I just dismissed it as bruised egos of sore losers. As they say, "boys will be boys."

I was almost home when I heard a guy say, "well, if it isn't the MVP." I looked around and saw a guy from the game. I responded "yep, that's me." The guy walked up to give me a high five. He began to question some of my basketball moves and the origin of my love for the game. I stopped to continue the conversation with the guy.

We were having a decent conversation until he said he could convert me. I responded, "Convert me from what to what?" He responded, "from a dike to a real woman." Before I could finish my returned response of "I am a real woman." The guy grabbed the jacket I was wearing and snatched it down over my arms while pinning me against a nearby tree. I was startled at how quick and calculating his movement was. I then responded, "What are you talking about, I am not gay."

The guy started kissing on me. I admit, it felt good and I thought he was rather cute. I pushed back against the guy and said, "No, let me go." With his free hand, he began to pull his penis out of his shorts. He then pushed me down to the ground with him on top of me. I screamed "No!!" again. He climbed on to my chest, with my arms still restrained by my own jacket and shoved his penis in my mouth.

I did attempt to fight him back to include biting him. When I bit him, he jumped up, called me a gay bitch and left me. After he left, I just at there under the tree and stared into the darkness. So many thoughts were running through my mind but I could not move. I felt frozen. Frozen to the point of being numb. All I wanted to do was play basketball.

I walked home feeling confused. I believe my thoughts were on a level higher beyond confused. I did not speak to anyone at my home, I just waved on my way to the bathroom. I got in the shower and scrubbed my face and body. I let the water run in my mouth and spit, over and over for about fifteen minutes. My thoughts ran back and forth.

I questioned why he chose me to sexually assault. I wondered why he felt so comfortable with his tactics? I also asked myself why my appearance was such a concern of his? Why was the suspicion of my sexually such a concern for him? Why did he feel compel to convert what he believed to be my sexuality? Who was he to convert or punish me for his suspicion?

As I ruminated on the event of my assault and the thoughts of why this could have possibly happened, I felt my blood boil. I was getting more and more angry about all of this.

> *Why was the suspicion of my sexually such a concern for him? Why did he feel compel to convert what he believed to be my sexuality?*

At this point in my life, I was beginning to feel like I was targeted. Really, all the signs pointed towards me being targeted because of suspicion. The suspicion of my sexual preference. First, why is it anyone's business besides mine? Secondly, how does a person qualify as the punisher of another due mainly to their unqualified thoughts?

This entire event changed everything in me, the mild mannered, unconfrontational, easy to blush young girl. I had become overly cautious of people and I heavily scrutinize my environment. I no longer feel completely safe around anyone. I believe my feelings are justified because I was violated in the realm, I felt the safest in...my safe haven of playing basketball.

After the event, I never went back to the park to play basketball. As much as I needed it, I just could not out-play the memories that had been attached to the outlet I once had.

After some time had passed, a few of my guy friend asked why I they had not seen me playing basketball in the park? Wow! Just this one question made my mind speed up by 3000 rpms. I instantly began to wonder if they knew what happened... I wondered if their inquiries laced in concern where merely jabs at my situation which in turn pierced the deepest part of my soul.

I was at a juncture where I could not distinguish real concern from someone being nosey. Having my outlet and my ability to choose my outcome taken from me was having a damaging effect on me. I was extremely irritable and short tempered. I had become highly suspicious...of everyone. After my assault, I no longer believed words. I only believed actions. Everyone had to earned my trust all over again.

I could actually see myself changing and out of fear, I could not do anything to stop it. This was not the me I recognized. This was not the me anyone knew me as. This me gave short responses and distanced herself. Yes, I was shy but not to the point of avoidance. I did not mind talking or being around others, I just would not initiate the process. If someone took the time to talk to me, I would open up and talk to their ear off. This was then...not any more.

The new me that had been created that I could not control, curve, or modify was a creation of protection. My subconscious had built a persona to give me the protection from opening myself for hurt. I would get up from bed as usual to a new day. I would look in the mirror and not see the me I was used too. There was a small glimmer of her in the smallest part of my eyes. I could see her. She was alone and afraid. To make this long story a tad shorter, this new me continued for a long time and the anger grew profusely.

In comes the popular crew. The girls who everyone looked as the ones with promised. The promise to always be good. The promise to always be successful. The promise that everyone took them for their word. The promise that they would always make the best decisions. What they really were a bunch of mean girls who threw rocks and hid their hands. They were the girls that protected the ones in their group who were just as crooked as they were. I saw them. Was that good enough for them? Nooooo, that would most certainly be asking for too much.

You would think by now, they would have grown to accept my appearance but no. It remained a conversation piece as well as ammunition for them to use against me. Their intent was to ambush me with me. Not today Satan. You were not going to get the chance to attack me without retaliation.

They all stood in ear shot and spoke at me. Just like I changed my name to remain anonymous. I will not include theirs either. I will just give them numbers. #2 said, "Oh boy, what are you reading?" #1 said, "who are you talking about?" #2 said, "I was talking about the boy/girl

Channel Austin

or whatever she is." By now, you should overstand why I called her #2 although she was the first to speak.

I did not respond to them. I guess they thought I did not hear them. I heard them. They waited a minute and then moved closer. #2 turned around right at my ear and in all of her dramatic effect repeated, "oh boy, what are you reading?" Although, I knew she was referring to me, I did not answer because I am not a boy. I knew and she knew exactly what she was doing when she phrased her comment in the way that she did. I bet she sat up all night trying to come up with a way to directly, indirectly call me a boy.

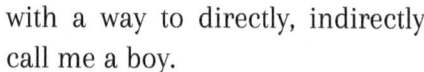

You would think by now, they would have grown to accept my appearance but no. It remained a conversation piece as well as ammunition for them to use against me. Their intent was to ambush me with me. Not today Satan.

She then grabbed at my book and I snatched away from her. She responded "Whew! Someone has their Fruit of The Looms in a bunch." I turned to her and responded, "I am not a boy, I am a girl. I don't wear Fruit of The Loom because girls do not wear boy's underwear. So, leave me alone". #2 mimicked me... "I'm a girl, leave me alone". Then she looked me deep in my eyes and said, "Well, we can see that the testosterone levels spike in the heat." That was it! I could not stand any more of her, well, their ridicule and messiness. I snatched her ponytail hair piece off her head and said, "This may be true but you are baldheaded in all temperatures." #2 screamed, grabbed her head and tried to get her ponytail from me. Everyone was laughing while I shifted her ponytail back and forth in the air as she jumped for it. Just when I was about to give it back to her, she said, "Give it to me, you gay bitch". When she said that, her words took me back to that night. When I bit the guy, who assaulted me on his penis, that's what he called me.

When she said that it was like the world stood still for about 30 seconds. I then turned and ran with her ponytail in my hand. The other kids were laughing so hard. I knew she could not catch me so I just teased ran and let her chase me. I saw a ditch with some water in it. I called out to #2 and said, "Look!" as I pointed to the ditch. She screamed, "You better not". I took her threat as a personal challenge and I "slammed dunked" her ponytail piece in the ditch water. Then I turned to her and said, "Oh boy, looks like your hair can't swim." #2 stopped and looked in horror. She then said, "I am going to beat your gay ass when I get my hands on you." She just continued to say the wrong things to me.

Once again, I felt myself getting even more angry with her. I reached down and grabbed the ponytail out of the ditch and I dunked it over and over, again. As soon as #2 got close to me, I threw the soaked hair piece at her and requested that she come beat my ass. I told her, "My ass is not gay but you can still come and try to beat it."

#2 just stood there and started crying. For some reason, I felt bad for her and vindicated all at one time. Going forward, I never had any other issues with #2 and her crew and #2 was never the same. Now we both belonged to the damaged club. What I surmised from this situation is that Hurt people, hurt people.

~

The Primary Author's Conclusion:

In this chapter, the matter of consent was the underlying subject. The term consent is defined as the permission for something to happen or agreement to do something. In this case, we are referring to consent to sexual activity. To have consent is to have obtain an affirmed agreement or yes to sexual engagement.

An absence of a "no" does not mean "yes." Consent must be active to truly be consent. A past "yes" does not constitute a present or current "yes".

Consent cannot be used as an unlimited component. Initial consent of kissing, is not consent for sexual activity. Participating in a relationship is not an automatic consent to sexual activity. Arguments in support of Rape Culture are not consents for sext to include using a person's attire as a justification for consent to have sexual activity. Nor does not fighting back equate to consent for sexual activity.

The Secrets We Keep

The Secrets We Keep

By

Shivonne Rachelle Arradondo

One of the hardest things I have ever had to do, was to tell this story. It was a constant reminder of the secrets we keep. My story begins in Tucumcari, New Mexico. I grew up on the North side of town and was part of the North Side gang. The members were like family. I was the second to the oldest, with one older brother and two younger brothers. At the time, I did not have biological sisters but I considered my female first cousins as my sisters. We did so much together from birthday parties, family gatherings, in school and church. I had a happy childhood with a respectable upbringing.

At age 5, I started to notice how some of my non-blood male cousins would look at me. It always made me feel uncomfortable. I can remember going to the park on the Northside and some of the older children would play hide-and-go-get-it. It is a game where the children hide and when found, you get the choice of a kiss or a touch somewhere on the body. The younger children were not allowed to play this game. Growing up, I was more of a tomboy who played sports with the boys so this game was of no interest to me. In my own tomboyish ways, I took pleasure in playing with dump trucks, my big wheel, footballs, basketballs and sometimes dolls.

The first time I was inappropriately touched, I was with my sister Raina. My cousin Anthony would pay us a quarter to sit on his lap. While sitting on his lap, he would move his hips in a circular motion to give himself an erection. All I really wanted was the quarter so I could purchase candy. He would then tell us it was a secret and if we told anyone, we would receive a spanking. Being a child and not knowing any better, I was afraid of spankings. This became a routine occurrence whenever he would see us, continuing until I was 7 years of age.

> While sitting on his lap, he would move his hips in a circular motion to give himself an erection.

During this time, my sisters Raina and Porsha moved away, leaving me hurt and sad. The molestation took on a new role with my non-blood cousins Saint, Johnnie and Shawn. As time passed, my body began to develop rather early, drawing more attention to my body. My "cousins" always wanted to play house with me but I did not want to play. I was more interested in visiting my Aunt Pearl and Uncle Solomon's house. They had younger daughters named Jackie and Paula. They were the sisters to Saint, Johnnie, and Shawn.

I enjoyed being at my Aunt Pearl and Uncle Solomon's because of the time they spent with me. They taught me how to play dominoes. This was the best part of going to their home. They would always open up their home to everyone. I would usually ask to stay over-night unaware of the nightmares that awaited me.

My "cousins" turned an innocent game of hide and seek into a game of molestation. Their game, called hide and go-get it, included touching me inappropriately. The silenced me by threatening that my parents would spank me if they knew about this. I did not like what they were doing to me but my fear kept me silent. Although, I enjoyed spending time with Jackie and Paula, it could not happen without their brothers being around.

This placed me in a difficult position to manage as a young child.

This placed me in a difficult position to manage as a young child. The pressure seemed endless I could not enjoy spending time with my girl cousins because my boy cousins felt compelled to touch me inappropriately. I could not stop them from touching me for fear of being spanked. I was constantly in a fearful state so, the molestation continued.

With every visit, the episodes of molestation would transition to many different places. Sometimes outside the house between the cinder block clothes line, on the side of the apartments, or in bedroom closets. There seem to be no where safe for my childhood innocence. I just wanted to play. I just wanted to spend time with my cousins without being touched.

At age 8, another one of my non-blood cousins, named Carl was asked to babysit my two younger brothers and myself. I felt comfortable with this because he had watched us before without incident. I should have known it was too good to be true, because as soon as my mother left with other family members, the molestation monster appeared.

Carl told me to pull down my panties and show him my vagina and if I did not, he would leave us alone at the house. My brothers were younger so they did not know or understand what was going on. However, we all understood the fear of being left alone at the apartment. I told Carl no and that I did not want to do this, and he actually left us alone at the apartment. He was just hiding outside on the side of the apartment but, we did not know this. I had to let him touch my vagina with his fingers so that he would not leave me and my brothers at the apartment. Carl told me that if I told on him,

I would get a spanking with the electric extension cord. This will be the last time that Carl would babysit myself and my brothers.

I told my mother that he kept leaving the apartment and she said she would never let him babysit us again. I was still afraid to tell my mother and father what these relatives were doing to me. I never showed signs of being molestation (as far as I was aware of) to my parents. My grades were good and my behavior was the same. I just felt that they would eventually get tired touching me.

> *They shut the door and told me that we were going to play a game and to pull down my panties.*

At age 9, I spent the night with Porsha and Jackie one night because my parents were going out to the Club LA. As soon as my Aunt Pearl and Uncle Solomon went to sleep, Saint and Johnnie made me come to their room. They shut the door and told me that we were going to play a game and to pull down my panties. I got upset and asked them to ask Porsha and Jackie to play too, but they said that they already did and it was my turn. They then took out their penis and said they were going to make a sandwich. I was more afraid than I had ever been because they had never taken it this far.

One brother was penetrating me from the back and the other from the front. The younger of the two wanted to try but there was nowhere else to enter me. It hurt and I wanted them to stop, so I started crying and begging them to stop and I was getting louder and they told me to be quiet. I continued to cry louder because the pain was unbearable. They finally stopped.

Fortunately, they were unsuccessful in fully penetrating me. I pulled my panties up and ran out of the room. I jumped in the bed, pulling the covers over my head and cried myself to sleep. I was awakened in the middle of the night by Saint trying to touch me and

I kept telling him to leave me alone. He saw that I was being too loud and would awaken his sisters, so he left. Early that morning, he came back and succeeded at touching me. On his way out the room, his older sister Melanie caught him. She told Auntie Pearl that she saw Saint coming out of his little sister's room? I was then awakened and asked what Saint was doing in the room. I acted as if I did not know what to say. It didn't go any further. How I wish I had the courage to have told my parents what these monsters had done to me. That was the worst of my childhood molestation. It was also the last time I stayed overnight.

Shortly after this part of my life, my family moved to Hobbs, NM. I was no longer being molested but the damage was already done. I was beginning to experience flashbacks, and nightmares of the molestation experiences. This was also the beginning of me learning to block out the memories of the trauma I had experienced.

Age 15, it was our first family reunion in Lubbock, TX. My sister Reina and I were outside greeting the family members as they showed up. I was waiting for my oldest brother to arrive because I hadn't seen him in a long time. Finally, my brother was here and as I saw him getting out of the car, he was followed by Saint. Seeing Saint made me physically ill. The sight of him, caused me to relive everything I had experienced because of him. I hugged my brother, but I dared not hug Saint. I was still afraid of him. My parents were not able to attend this reunion, so I went inside and right away my uncle Dodge (known as my "PA") asked me to come to his bedroom to talk. Although I was afraid, I told him what my "cousins" had done to me. My Uncle wanted to do something bad to him, but decided it was not in the best interest right now. He assured my safety and said no one was going to touch me while he was around. He promised me that I would no longer see Saint after this reunion. My uncle warned me to avoid being around Saint, while we were here as well as, to inform him if he tried anything inappropriate.

Shivonne Rachelle Arradondo

During the entire duration of the family reunion, I kept giving evil stares to Saint. I found myself wishing the neighboring pit bull dogs would jump the fence and tear him apart. This wish was not just for Saint, it was for every sick person that molested me. I felt my "cousins" took advantage of my naiveness and I wanted them all to suffer the same fate. Thankfully, the reunion ended without any incidents.

As I grew up, I was not aware of how much these experiences would affect my life. The experiences, the flashbacks, and the nightmares affected my relationships with me. I found myself wanting less and less contact with men. I had decided that I really did not want to be touched by any man. I felt that all men were meant to hurt me in some form or fashion. As I continued in to womanhood, I was fortunate to experience love. This love helped me to not think about the trauma I had experienced as a child. Learning about and experiencing love helped me manage my thoughts and feelings of my past.

After completing my AIT military training at the age of 19, I returned to Lubbock, Texas. I then enrolled in Texas Tech University. I met this guy named Melvin who lived in the college dorms next to mine. Melvin was a Senior and I was a Freshman. One night there was an off-campus party that we went to together. There was a lot of drinking. I only had one drink that Melvin brought to me. The drink made me unstable and I became quickly dizzy. Melvin escorted me to one of the bedrooms. After this, the only thing I remember was waking up partially naked. Still unsure of the occurrence but frighten something was wrong. Melvin was in the restroom and he came out talking about how good I was.

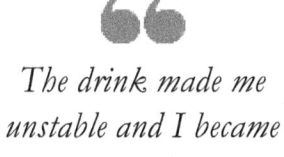

The drink made me unstable and I became quickly dizzy.

I did not give Melvin consent to touch me. I was not aware at the time but I had been drugged and raped. The only thing I could do at the time was find my clothing and get out of there. Ashamed and confused, I left in tears.

Due to past fears making their way into my current state, I decided against going to the police. I felt that something was put in my drink but I knew I could not prove it. I went to see the doctor because I was so affected by this that they wanted to prescribe me antidepressants. I never took the pills. Whenever the thought of what had happened to me would cross my mind, I would drink that memory away.

Having a job and going to college, I had to manage my drinking so I would not drink all day. I made up for it on Fridays and Saturdays. This was my coping mechanism. Even with my constant thoughts of suicide, I was determined not to seek professional help. I had to find a way to survive this. I began to limit my drinking and increase my interactions with friends. I just wanted to have a good time. I just wanted to live life and be happy.

I was pregnant with twins but miscarried one of the babies at 4 months at the age of 20. When I gave birth to my first child and my life changed dramatically. This was new to me, I had someone would not hurt me and would love me unconditionally. I was overprotective of my baby. I wanted to ensure no one would ever touch my baby the way they touched me when I was younger. I became even more protective when I gave birth to my second child. I was blessed with one boy and three girls. My children became my coping mechanism for any childhood or adult trauma that I had suffered.

Shivonne Rachelle Arradondo

> **" "**
> *This is where my PTSD really began to affect me.*

Growing older and living my life, I experienced marriage, divorce, and a few long-time relationships. I found myself not wanting to be touched again by any man. This even affected my relationship with my father. I did not share any of this with my parents until I was in my 40s; I am now 48. A couple years ago, I received social media friend requests from my molesters. This caused me have flashbacks of the past experiences that robbed of my innocence for years. This is where my PTSD really began to affect me.

As an adult, I now know that these people were horrible, sick and twisted. Their requests, stirred up everything I had worked so hard to forget. I started thinking back to being a child and being mad at myself for not having the courage to tell my parents about what was being done to me. Had I told my parents, I know for a fact, that those stole my innocence through molestation would no longer be around. My parents would have made sure of this although doing so would have landed them in prison.

Although, the experiences I have left me with traumatic challenges I have to work through. I am so thankful that the molestation did not inhibit me from bearing children of my own. My children are one of my greatest assets.

As I reflect back on being molested and raped, I now know it was and still is illegal for those types of acts to occur. They're criminal and punishable up to prison time. I encourage those of you who may have experienced being molested or raped to seek guidance on therapy and treatment. There are many resources available to offer assistance. Other great coping mechanism are support groups because you will be amongst your peers.

I remember thinking prayer would provide me all the help I needed but learned that God works through other people, as well.

Please know that you are not alone because you are amongst many who cannot speak. I feel it is my mission to be that voice for those who cannot speak.

In my opinion, molesters should be punished and not able to continue to do this to other children. The same goes for the men who sexually assault adults. When we are silent, we give those types of people the opportunity to go and do this to someone else. When you do not report the sexual assault, it demonstrates how the secrets we keep, can ruin our lives. Tell me your story and I will be your voice.

~

Primary Author's Conclusion:

In this chapter, the matter of molestation was the underlying subject. There are instances where a person does not have the ability to legally give consent. These instances include, someone being under the age of legal consent, someone lacking the mental capacity (due to disability or illness), lacking physical ability (asleep, passed out, drugged, drunk, or high), or under duress such as being threatened, manipulated, coerced, or forced into agreeing.

A Life Restored

A Life Restored

By

Colin Jefferies

The world sheds tears with the victims. The world hurts in the same vein as the ones who have been hurt. The world feels the anger with the ones who have been angered. The world shares the pain of the ones who have been pained. The world shouts vengeance towards the culprit in support of the mistreated.... As well, we should.

My heart cries for anyone who has been violated, taken advantage of and the worst of all, sexually assaulted or raped. It is hard to believe that anyone would intentionally inflict pain and hurt on another person without remorse. It is even more difficult to believe that someone would actually commit such an offense several times.

As I mentioned, my heart cries along with the aggrieved but my mind often wonders why the accused who have been found innocent do not receive the same support? Where are the support systems for the alleged who were actually not guilty? Who sheds tears for them beside the family members who experienced the incident with them? Who promises vengeance in support of them? Why are there not stiffer penalties and jail time for those who falsely accuse others of sexual assault and rape?

Colin Jefferies

> *False accusations and false charges of sexual assault kill personal character. False accusations kill careers. False accusations kill relationships. False accusations kill families.*

False accusations and false charges of sexual assault and rape are deadly. False accusations and false charges of sexual assault kill personal character. They kill careers. They kill relationships. They kill families. They kill hopes and dreams of better. They kill assets. They kill opportunities. They kill trust. They even kill the will of the falsely accused.

The pain of being falsely accused of a crime as serious as sexual assault and rape is a hard one to describe. Even if, you are found not guilty and it is proved that you did not do what you were accused of, your life is never the same. Your life is never the same because people still connect the incident with you. People still mention that you were accused, charged, and jailed for rape but then say…it was proved he did not do it. My question is why can't you lead with the truth and leave it there. Why does it have to be at the end of the conversation. How about saying. "He was accused but did not do it and was found not guilty. Why not lead your introduction of me with who I am to you. Say there's Christopher, he's a nice guy (the end). All of the other stuff is not necessary nor does it help me in getting my life back.

The consequences of being falsely accused ruins lives. All of the support is given to the victims and trust me I get that but rarely do you hear of any support given to the ones accused and found not guilty. Rarely do we hear of the injustices and sorrow they face after such an experience. They are left to fight this battle alone and it rarely ends well.

Asking that support be given to those falsely accused should not cause a war or divide us. Even with the corruption in our justice system or the one sidedness of the system, it says, innocent until

THE INVISIBLES

PROVEN guilty. If this is true, why have we developed a mindset to believe anyone who states they have been sexually assaulted with out proof. Why is it that their word is enough?

Asking that support be given to those falsely accused should not cause a war or divide us.

Please know I am not speaking the aspect of

Blaming, shaming, and disbelief of anyone who has actually been sexually assaulted or raped. I am speaking from the aspect of a person who WAS falsely accused and charged with rape that subsequently placed me in jail. I was arrested and jailed on the charge of rape when I had not raped anyone. I was arrested and charged because a woman said I did and was believed despite me saying I did not. Where was my support and due process? I will tell you where it was... nowhere to be found. I was embarrassed and arrested at my job. I was handcuffed in front of my boss and co-workers. I was not allowed to call anyone or granted any understanding.

There is a division of those who believe guilty until proven innocent in rape and those who believe innocent until proven guilty in every case, whether it is rape or not. This is the world I was living in and there were more people on the side of seeing me as guilty. I found myself pinching myself because I was in total disbelief. I was a good guy. I am a good guy. I was the guy you wanted your sister or daughter to date. I am still the guy you would want your sister or daughter to date.

I was raised in a good family. I was never in any type of trouble. I made good grades in school. I went to college, had good grades, graduated and got a great job. I have dated many women and had lengthy relationships, with no issues. When we were together, we were together. When we decided we no longer wanted to be together, we parted amicably. As I mentioned, I have never been in any trouble, not so much as a speeding ticket. Absolutely nothing.

That was until I met Karen. Karen was beautiful. Karen was outgoing and loquacious. Karen was also an opportunist. I met Karen at a happy hour and discovered we worked for the same company but in different areas. It seemed that we hit it off (got alone, was a good fit) instantly. As I sat there at the bar listening to Karen speak, I was thinking that I wanted to see her again. While Karen was talking about her fur-babies Molly and Mimi, I asked if she would join me on a date the following day. Karen said "Yes" and went right back into her story about her dogs.

> *Even with the corruption in our justice system or the one sidedness of the system, it says, innocent until PROVEN guilty.*

A few hours later, I informed Karen I was about to leave but could not wait to see her on tomorrow for our date. Karen said she was leaving too. I walked her to her car and she suggested I follow her home. I did. This was where my life began to spiral downward.

Karen invited me in her apartment. As soon as the door was shut, she began kissing me. I initially pushed back because I needed her to recognize that she initiated this. She smiled at me and began to kiss me again. From here, I was fine because she had proven to me that this was what she desired. Karen then kissed me lower and lower (I'm sure you get the point). We were still at the door. While she was performing oral sex on me, I was thinking, I sure chose the right woman to talk to tonight! It was just that good.

Karen led me to her bedroom. We passed through the rooms in her apartment going to bedroom so quick, that to this day, I could not tell you what her place looks like. We both got undressed and climbed in her bed. We kissed and began to have consensual sex until we simply could not any more. The next day, I had car issues

THE INVISIBLES

and I cancelled the date. I told her that we could grab lunch the following week. Karen got very angry that I was cancelling the date. She offered to drive but I was really turned off by her anger and said no. As a man, I just did not feel right with her having to pick me up for a date. Furthermore, I figured my car repairs would only take a few days.

On Monday morning, I received a visit to my office by my boss and two police. I had absolutely no idea, why they were there. I was asked to stand up and move from behind my desk. I did. With all of the cop shows I have watched over the course of my life, I could not phantom what was about to happen next. Then, I heard one of the police say, "Turn around and place your hands behind your back." I responded. "what?"

The police grabbed my arms and placed handcuffs on my wrists. I was read my rights and told I was being arrested for an alleged rape. I had heard people say, "they saw their life pass before their eyes" but I had never experienced it for myself, until now.

With all of the cop shows I have watched over the course of my life, I could not phantom what was about to happen next.

I was walked out my office in handcuffs, escorted by the police in front of everyone. This was the most embarrassing thing I had ever experience. I was so confused and shocked that I forgot to asked who it was they were claiming I had raped. It became painstaking real to me when they placed me in the backseat of the car and closed the door. I recalled looking out the window at my car in the parking lot as we drove by. I finally snapped to myself and asked the police who the person was?

The police pulled out his notepad and said Karen Stahl (name changed in this book). All I could hear was the name Karen ringing in my head because I truly did not know her last name. I responded,

"No, this cannot be!" "I did not rape her!" The police reminded me of my rights to remain silent.

From that day to this day, I spent 4 years behind bars in jail. We went to court. There was no conclusive evidence even linking me to her other than her statements. I was afraid for the outcome of my case not because I was guilty because I was not. I was afraid because I was a Black man and Karen was a white woman. I was afraid because her white tears held more weight than my stellar reputation. Her white fragility and white tears held more weight than my Black truth. Regardless of what I said, she was seen as the innocent victim. Even after I told them how she initiated the sexual act from the time we set foot inside her apartment, it did not compel to her accusing me of rape. I even remember noticing one of the polices smirk when I talked about the sexual encounter but yet, he led me right to a jail cell.

Day after day, I sat in that jail trying to figure out what I could say to make them believe me. I sat there and pondered as to who I could contact to help me. With all of the thinking I was doing, I could not come up with anything that could assist me in this matter. I went so far as to ask the police if a rape kit was done. He smiled and said, I am sure it was. Now I was left to wonder if I would be framed with the rape kit. No one tries to understand the maltreatment and lack of justice experienced by Black people when hey have been accused of a crime. All I could think of was the fact that the rape kit could either save me or finish killing me. I settled with the fact that it would probably finish killing me because I knew I had been there at one time. However, being there at some point does not mean I raped her.

I sat there in that jail trying to piece all of the pieces together. Why would she accuse me of such a heinous crime? I remember thinking...We met on a Friday evening. We had sex the same night. We were supposed to go out the next day but my car was out of service. I went through every second of our sexual experience to see if there was something I missed. I did this other and over, every day and could not find the link as to why she would do this. I was finally

THE INVISIBLES

given a bond that was unaffordable. My parents put their house up to secure my bond. I was let out until my court day.

The weight I felt as I walked out of that jail was something I had never felt in my life. The despair I felt was like a carrying a boulder around on my back while having a clamp on my chest. I felt so weak. I felt so damaged. I felt hopeless.

Her white fragility and white tears held more weight than my Black truth. Regardless of what I said, she was seen as the innocent victim.

As I reflected over my life, I could not think of one solitary thing I have done wrong that would be worth the punishment I was receiving. To say the absolute least, I was livid. I was so angry to the point of rage but, there was nothing I could do to change this. I had so many emotions running simultaneously running through me. I wanted to tear up and break up everything in sight. I wanted to scream. I wanted to run. I wanted to cry...so, I did.

Prior to going home, I went to visit my parents. I just needed to experience safety and love. I walked in my parent's home. I could see the pain in my mother's eyes. She ran to me and hugged me. I felt like I was six years old and had fallen off my bike. I wanted my mother to have the ability to hug and kiss the pain away, as she had done countless times when I was growing up. I have not met anyone physically, who can take away my pain and make me fell whole again, like my mother. I needed her to make the pain to go away. I needed her to tell me it was going to be ok and that it would actually be ok.

My father stood beside us with his hand on my mother's shoulder and then with his massive arms, embraced us both. It was then that I came completely unglued. I believe I loss consciousness for a few minutes. My parents moved me over to the couch. I cried so hard. I mean a deep internal cry that manifested to the outside. I laid there with my head on my mother's lap and my father's hand on my back. I could feel the strength of my heavenly father move within me through my parents. I was beginning to feel better and stronger. Although there was no evidence that my situation had changed, I believed it was at that moment, it truly did. I could feel my father praying and my mother moaning, yet, no words were spoken.

I raised up from my mother's lap and said to them both. I have a hellava fight on my hands, but I was determined to keep fighting. I walked them through the entire night. I told them every single detail. I ended with, "I am innocent. I did not rape Karen, it was consensual." Both of my parent's stated they believed me and that they never doubted my innocence.

> *My attorney responded, "I do not believe that you did but, we have to go through the process."*

The next day, I drove to my apartment in Philly. Initially, I just sat in my car, not wanting to get out. I quickly picked up my feelings and got out. I had to believe that if I was going to fight, I had to be strong from every angle. I walked inside my apartment and immediately called my attorney. I asked him if he had received the results from the rape kit. My attorney said, "No, the results may take months." I remember screaming "Months?" "Why would it take that long?" "This is really my only saving grace against this she said situation."

My attorney responded, "Well, rape is a serious charge." I responded, "I understand that and as well it should be." "Trust me, I do not take the notion of rape, lightly. It's just that I did not rape her." My attorney responded, "I do not believe that you did but, we have to go through the process." Every negative thought I could think of came rushing in on me. It was all fine and well that he did not believe I did it but, what was he doing to help me prove that I did not do it? This was the beginning of my "The world is against me, the disbelief tour."

THE INVISIBLES

I say this because, everyone I encountered from that day on stated they never believed I raped her. All of this verbal confidence was great to hear but it did nothing for my case.

After a few days of rest and mental anguish, I figured I would go talk to the supervisor at my job. To my surprise, I was stopped by the security personnel and told I had to leave the premises. I could not believe what was happening. I asked the security guard to contact my supervisor to come to the front to speak to me. After a short wait, the manager, not the supervisor showed up. He explained that I was no longer employed there and because my accuser worked there, I could not be within a certain amount of feet of her. He requested my badge.

Placing my employee badge in his hand was a difficult move for me. All I could think was, these people know me. I have worked here for years and they just abandoned me as if I was no one. I was "hot" and disappointed. I turned and walked out the front doors of the company. To the right of me, I saw two ladies begin to whisper to each other...so, the whispers had started. To be honest, I don't know if they were whispering about me but, it sure felt like they did not feel the need to whisper until they saw me. I began to tally up my losses. I had lost my freedom. I lost my stellar reputation. I had lost my good job, that allowed me to afford my good life. I had lost my ability to not believe every whisper was about me and my situation. So, I guess I had lost my peace too.

If it was not for the love and support, I was receiving from my parents, I am sure I would not have made it this far. My court case was to be in fourteen months. Just what the hell was I supposed to do for myself for the next fourteen months? I began avoiding people and places. I would just sit in my apartment...and drink. One day while sitting, thinking, and drinking, I noticed a flashing light on my counter. It was the light on my voicemail. I remember I had not checked my voicemails since I had been released. I had several voicemails from my friends (that I cannot seem to get a return call back from since my release.) I had several hang up voicemails and some where the caller just wasted space by sitting there and not saying anything. I finally heard a voicemail that simply said "I am sorry. I never dreamed that this would go as far as it has. I really like you and just wanted things to finally work out for me in a relationship."

I could not believe my ears...There I was sitting in a sinkhole that was dug for me, where everything I have worked for had spiraled out of my reach. There I was sitting in my apartment, drinking myself to death because of the pain that had been inflicted on me. There I was listening to a message from Karen, my accuser, telling me she was sorry.

I have a hellava fight on my hands, but I was determined to keep fighting.

I slapped the phone system off my counter. The unadulterated gall of her to call me and apologize after she put me in this situation. I remember screaming "Sorry!" Sorry!" Did she think this was some type of game? She was playing with my life!! This situation had turned my life completely around. I had a fairly good life, with a decent livelihood. Because of her accusation, I lost everything and have to now work in my family's business because I cannot find a decent job. I agree that yes, she is sorry, alright. A Sorry individual who has ruined my life because she could not get her way.

After stomping around my apartment, knocking things over, and arguing my case before an invisible jury, I realized I had her on recording. I called my attorney and told him about the voicemail message. Let down once again, he informed me that there was no way to prove that the voice on the voicemail was hers. When I tell you that this knocked the win out of me. I literary, fell to my knees and begged him to fix this. My attorney responded, "I wish I could but I cannot. We will have to let this play itself out. In the following months, I went through disappointment after disappointment. It appeared that there was no hope in the truth coming out and me winning my case. The final straw for me happened three months prior to my court date.

While working in my family business, a family friend came by with her niece. I had known this woman all of my life and she was always considered a voice of reason. She went on to tell me how when she heard about my plight that she did not believe not one word of it because she knew my character. She told me how much she had been praying for me and my family. She even assured me that this would be worked out and I would be fine because God had my back. This was great to hear and it even made me feel better. After she had taken care of her business, she informed us of her pending departure of our business. When I walked up to hug her bye and to tell her how much better she made me feel, in a subtle but apparent way, she moved her niece out of my reach.

In a subtle but apparent way, she moved her niece out of my reach.

I could not believe my eyes, but it was true. With everything she had said to include how she did not believe any of what was said, she showed me she did not truly believe me. She even told me she had been praying for me. Now, I am wondering just what the hell was she praying. When I saw what she did, I stopped and gave her a long look then I turned and walked away. She walked out too. Since my release, I had noticed that several people went out of their way to avoid me. Their avoidance did not bear the same level of hurt, as it did coming from a close family friend. I discovered that many would rather run with a lie opposed to riding with the truth. This hurt me on a level so deep in my soul that it is unexplainable.

My attorney called one and a half months before my court date. It was a phone call I would never forget. I answered the phone and plopped down on my couch because I was never sure of the outcomes of our phone conversations. My attorney said, "the rape case was found not to be inclusive of your DNA." I responded, "I did not believe it would because, we had sex on a Friday night and she accused me on the following Monday morning." My attorney said, "Let me finish, the rape case was found not to be inclusive of your DNA but it did include someone else's." I jumped straight up from my seated position on my couch a said, "What?" My attorney said, "Yes."

I was so excited and relieved but mostly uncertain because I was not sure how this would benefit my case. My attorney told me that he could not promise me anything but my case was not looking much better for me. I responded great and he told me he would be in touch. The events of case began to move fast. After receiving the rape kit results, the DA investigated everything around the findings. Through this investigation, Karen admitted that I did not rape her. She also admitted that she had sexual intercourse with another man in less than 48 hours after our sexual encounter. The rape charges were dropped.

I was physically free but my reputation was now tainted. I now had a record and was registered as a sex offender. I had to pay additional money to work towards having the charges expunged from my record. I had spent thousands of thousand of dollars trying to protect my innocence. My parents had put their home that they had worked hard to have and keep, up to cover the bond needed to get me out of jail. I lost my job that I had worked hard to secure. I lost my livelihood and almost my dignity over a lie. I could not see my life ever being the same. I was nit able to get my job back but I did gain an even more rewarding career as a counselor. I became an advocate for others like myself who have been falsely accused of sexual assault.

There is nothing that will give me back all of the time or sleep I lost behind this. There is nothing that will give me back the hurt and pain I felt. I am just so glad that my thoughts and actions were rooted in my parent's teaching which kept me from doing the unthinkable because, I thought of suicide every day. I had to rely on my parents because there is no support prior or even afterwards for people who are falsely accused. Regardless of what is said, the accused are deem guilty until proven innocent. There is no system in place to ensure the accused is given adequate opportunity to be proven not guilty prior to being jailed and subsequently losing everything they have. This in it self is unfair. As I have mentioned before, I believe the story of the accuser should be heard but I also believe the story of the accused should be as well. I believe anyone who commits a sexual assault should be punished and in the same vein, I also believe people who falsely make accusations of sexual assault be prosecuted.

~

Primary Author's Conclusion:

In this chapter, the matter of false accusations was the underlying subject. Allow me to begin by saying everyone should have the opportunity to share their story. I also believe no one should be degraded and made to feel that their experience is not of importance and does not matter. With all of this being believed, I also believe that no one should be falsely accused.

In the realm of fairness to all, the falsely accused should also have the opportunity to give their story without prejudgment. No one should be presumed guilty without proof. Even with all of the flaws within the justice system, no one should be convicted without due process and proof. According to Sir William Garrow (1760-1840), accusers should be robustly tested in court, which is commonly expressed in the phrase "presumed innocent until proven guilty " (Mueller & Kirkpatrick, 2009).

The Effects of Sexual Assault

Personal experiences and research have shown that sexual assault experiences have led to various psychological effects such as (PTSD) Post Traumatic Stress Disorder, depression, reduce mental health rigor and other secondary medical conditions (Jackson-Dean, 2017).

The increase of psychological and physical health issues among individuals who have experienced sexual assault, sexual harassment and even rape often leads to requiring some costly and time-consuming treatments (Jackson-Dean, 2020, Ditcher and True, 2015; Fitz-Charles, Drasgow, and Magley,1999; Turchik and Wilson, 2010; Willness, Steel, and Lee, 2017). All forms of sexual assault are much different than any other type of assault but like anything else, the responses may be situational and no doubt subjective.

The effects of sexual assault can be stem from the victim's subconsciously believing they are to blame for the act perpetrated against them. These beliefs produce feelings of guilt and mistrust. If the assault was from a relative or close friend, the victim may feel compelled to not tell anyone which can have overwhelming detrimental effects due to having to cope with the shrine of secrecy.

The effects of sexual assault can produce several psychological issues to include participating in painful self-inflicting acts. It has been discovered that many victims of sexual assault eased the pain they feel by hurting themselves; many researchers are in deliberations as to the official cause of this. According to Levenkron (1999), self-injury is a deliberate, non- suicidal behavior that inflicts physical harm on one's body to relieve emotional distress. Self-injury has a paradoxical effect in that the pain self-inflicted actually sets off an endorphin rush, relieving the self-harmer from deep distress.

Other psychological issues include panic attacks, sleeping disorders and even eating disorders. Panic attacks derive from episodes of overwhelming intense anxiety. The anxiety produced panic attacks can be activated by anything or even nothing. Panic attacks can be described as sudden difficulty breathing or even a sort of uncontrollable hyperventilating.

Sleeping disorders can range from the inability to sleep through an entire night. Sleeping disorders can also be described as having Somniphobia which is the fear of sleep. Some traumatized individuals suffer with Somniphobia challenges because they believe that sleeping limits their personal control of their safety. Nightmares and bad dreams can be an attributed effect of a sexual assault. Lack of sleep due to Somniphobia, nightmares, and sleep walking can have detrimental effects on not only a person's physical and mental health; but a decrease in quality of life as well. The bad dreams can also include day time flashbacks of the experiences. Nightmares and flashbacks can give the perception of reliving the sexual assault all over again.

The longer sleeping challenges are experienced, the more they contribute to chronic fatigue. Chronic fatigue is the constant feeling of tiredness and lack of rest. In the case of chronic fatigue, the body is in a state where it is so rest deprived leading to the unbalance of the circadian rhythm. Circadian rhythm effects the hormonal balance and bodily functions.

Suffers would be better served by seeking professional assistance for the these and other challenges attributed to sexual assault. Please review the list of organizations available to assist victims of sexual assault.

Sexual Assault Assistance

Director of Crime Victim Services- https://ovc.ojp.gov/directory-crime-victim-services

Health and Human Services- www.HHS.gov

Love Is Respect- https://www.loveisrespect.org/personal-safety/ 866-331-9474

National Assault Hotline- 800.656.HOPE (4673)

National Coalition Against Domestic Violence (NCADV) 303-839-1852

National Domestic Hotline- 800-799-SAFE (7233)

Safe Hotline- www.safehelpline.org 877-995-5247

References

Bergen, R. and Barnhill, E. (2006). Marital Rape: New Research and Directions; The National Online Resource Center on Violence Against Women; www.Vawnet.org/material/marital-rape-new-research-and-directions.

Fitzgerald, Louise F., Fritz Drasgow, Charles L. Hulin, Michele J. Gelfand, and Vicki J. Magley. (1997). "Antecedents and Consequences of Sexual Harassment in Organizations: A Test of an Integrated Model." *Journal of Applied Psychology* 82(4): 578–89. https://doi.org/10.1037/0021-9010.82.4.578.

Levenkron, S. (1999). Cutting: Understanding and overcoming self-mutilation. New York: W.W. Norton and Company.

McMahon-Howard, C.; Clay-Warner, J.; and Renzulli, L. (2009). Sociological Perspectives; Vol. 52, No. 4, pp. 505-531.

Mueller, Christopher B.; Kirkpatrick, Laird C. (2009). Evidence; 4th ed. Aspen (Wolters Kluwer). pp. 133-34.

Jackson-Dean, L. (2017). Seed To Seeds: Systemic Oppression and PTSD; pp. 53.

Jackson-Dean, L. (2020). The PIVOT Anthology: 20 Personal Experiences Of Experts Getting Out Of Their Own Way; pp. 96.

The Sexual Assault Victim Advocacy Center, INC, (2021). https://www.savacenterga.org/statistics

Willness, Chelsea, Piers Steel, and Kibeom Lee. 2007. "A Meta-Analysis of the Antecedents and Consequences of Workplace Sexual Harassment." *Personnel Psychology* 60(1): 127–62. https://doi.org/10.1111/j.1744-6570.2007.00067.x.

Biographies

~

Dr. LaShonda M. Jackson-Dean

Dr. LaShonda M. Jackson-Dean a Multiple National and International American Best-Seller Author of a variety of genres to include African American Studies, Women, Management, Militaristic, Motivational, Wellness, and Fitness Studies, Fiction as well as Non-fiction literature. She is a Multiple National and International Empowerment Speaker, Life, and Success Strategist. Dr. Jackson-Dean, an adjunct professor, and entrepreneur gives voice to the voiceless through her writings and speaking. She is the author of A Phenomenological Study of the Underrepresentation of Senior Level African American Women in Corporations, Seed to Seeds Systemic Oppression and PTSD, Level Up! Through Mindfulness, Level Up!

Through Mindfulness Life-Book Part II, A Tea Party and a Prayer (Children's Book), The PIVOT Anthology: 20 Personal Stories of Experts Getting Out Of Their Own Way, The Christmas Magic Of You (Children's Book), The Invisibles Anthology: Sexual Assault Awareness, future literary projects entitled The Adventures of Tike and Tunka (Children's Book) and The Invisible (4 Parts of a 5-Part Series). Dr. Jackson-Dean has Co-Authored five published collaborations (Gumbo for The Soul, Love Letters to My Girls, Women Win Against the Odds, I'm Speaking: rewritten Rules of Affirmation for Women Disruptors, and Break-Through) and is currently the primary Author in an Anthologies entitled The PIVOT (2020) and The Invisibles (2021) . She publishes through her own Publishing Company, Jackson-Dean Investments Publishing.

Dr. Jackson-Dean has had the honor of being a guest author and or speaker at several events to include a personal invite to the 2018 Congressional Black Caucus 48th Annual Legislative Conference and The Congress of Black Women Conference, both in Washington, DC. A guest speaker at TSU- Texas State University in 2019-2020 and a Guinness Book of World Records Speaker in 2020. Guest Speaker at The Champions Summit, The Level Up Summit, The Power Up Summit and The PIVOT Conference, all for 2021.

Dr. Jackson-Dean is the proud owner of her own TV Network (JDI Multi-Media Network) a Jackson-Dean Investments Company and producer of her own TV Show. The network is comprised of TV, Digital Streaming, Talk Shows, Podcasts, Education, Movies, Music, Mini-Series and Concerts. She provides a platform to assist others in creating their own TV shows and providing them a network to get their message to the masses. She is the host of two TV Talk Shows entitled Just So You Know Moment with a Twist and Just So You Know Moment with Dr. Jackson-Dean. The first talk show entails episodes of highlight conversation with business owners, community leaders, authors, speakers, Non-Profit Founders, and the like. Just So You Know Moment with a #Twist TV talk show premiered in February 2020. The second TV show, Just So You Know Moment with Dr.

Jackson-Dean, which is based on motivation, inspiration, and educational topics, first premiered in the Fall of 2018.

Dr. Jackson-Dean, is also a United States Air Force Disabled Veteran, provides coaching services through Jackson-Dean Professional Solutions to women, men, Veterans, women entrepreneurs, and those who aspire to greatness. She is the Founder and CEO of Greatness Pursued a Non-Profit Organization. The organization is committed to empowering Veteran women struggling with their transition from military to civilian life after surviving (MST) Military Sexual Trauma to a life successfully reaching life-changing goals.

Dr. Jackson-Dean holds a Doctorate of Management in Organizational Leadership, Masters of Business Administration (MBA); and a Bachelor of Science in Occupational Education specializing in Bio-Environmental Engineering, Minor in Business Administration. She holds several certifications from leading educational institutes, to include Harvard University, in leadership, professorship, management, and wellness. With well over twenty years of practical experience as a professional in research, entrepreneurship, and management, she provides solid discussions on various topics. Dr. Jackson-Dean educates through lectures, workshops, seminars, and special guest appearances.

To book Dr. LaShonda M. Jackson-Dean for your next speaking event please contact her publicist at Publicist.DrLJackson-Dean@gmail.com. To purchase any of her books, materials, and products visit her website, www.DrLaShondaJacksonDean.com, and www.JacksonDeanInvestments.com.

FaceBook: www.facebook.com/AuthorDrLaShondaJacksonDean

Twitter: www.twitter.com/DrLJD_Author

Instagram: www.instagram.com/DrLaShondaJacksonDean

LinkedIn:
http://bit.ly/2RONw0nDrLaShondaJacksonDeanLinkedInProfile
YouTube: http://bit.ly/38YjxZFDrJacksonDeanYouTubeChannel
Website: www.DrLaShondaJacksonDean.com
Booking email: Publicist.DrLJacksonDean@gmail.com
For TV Network Information:
Instagram.com/JDIMultiMediaNetwork
Facebook: www.facebook.com/TheTVTalkShowQueen
Facebook: www.facebook.com/JDIMultiMediaNetwork
www.JacksonDeanInvestments.com
Talk Show: Just So You Know Moment with A
JustSoYouKnowMomentWithATwist.com

If you are interested in co-authoring in a future Anthology, contact

Dr. LaShonda M. Jackson-Dean at DrLaShondaJacksonDean@gmail.com

For More Information.

Dr. LaShonda M. Jackson-Dean's Anthologies

Thank you for reading The Invisibles Anthology: Sexual Assault Awareness.

For your reading pleasures visit

www.DrLaShondaJacksonDean.com/shop .

Meet the Authors

Dr. LaShonda M. Jackson-Dean

(Primary Author)

Daisy Herman

(Co-Author)

Marjorie Calhoun

(Co-Author)

Shivonne Rachelle Arrandondo

(Co-Author)

Colin Jefferies

(Co-Author)

Channel Austin

(Co-Author)

www.ingramcontent.com/pod-product-compliance
Lightning Source LLC
Chambersburg PA
CBHW070514090426
42735CB00012B/2781